#LEADERSHIP**tweet**

140 Bite-Sized Ideas to Help You Become the Leader You Were Born to Be

By Kevin Eikenberry
Foreword by Chris Brogan

Copyright © 2009 by Kevin Eikenberry

All rights reserved. No patent liability is assumed with respect to the use of the information contained herein. Although every precaution has been taken in the preparation of this book, the publisher and author(s) assume no responsibility for errors or omissions. Neither is any liability assumed for damages resulting from the use of the information contained herein.

First Printing: November 2009

Paperback ISBN: 978-1-60773-062-0 (1-60773-062-6)

Place of Publication: Silicon Valley, California USA

Paperback Library of Congress Number: 2009939886

eBook ISBN: 978-1-60773-063-7 (1-60773-063-4)

Trademarks

All terms mentioned in this book that are known to be trademarks or service marks have been appropriately capitalized. Happy About® and its imprint, Super Star Press, cannot attest to the accuracy of this information. Use of a term in this book should not be regarded as affecting the validity of any trademark or service mark.

Warning and Disclaimer

Every effort has been made to make this book as complete and as accurate as possible, but no warranty of fitness is implied. The information provided is on an "as is" basis. The authors and the publisher shall have neither liability nor responsibility to any person or entity with respect to loss or damages arising from the information contained in this book.

Advance Praise

"Kevin Eikenberry has collected remarkable leadership tweets you can learn from and share."

Wally Bock @*WallyBock*, Author, Blogger, and Trainer

"Effective leadership calls for concise communication. Kevin has surely shown remarkable leadership here!"

Steve Roesler @*steveroesler*, Founder and Principal, The Steve Roesler Group, Award-Winning Blogger

---

"Kevin's collection of leadership tweets will inspire, encourage, challenge, and motivate you. His concise spot-on advice is a must read."

Becky Robinson @*LeaderTalk*, Blogger, LeaderTalk, Mountain State University

---

"On target...again! Kevin has a knack for converting complex ideas into easy-to-digest learning points. Bravo!"

Guy Harris *@recovengineer*, Owner, Principle Driven Consulting, Author, Blogger, Speaker, and Trainer

---

"Inspiration drives growth. The tweets in this book are a driving factor."

Kyle Lacy *@kyleplacy*, Co-founder and Business Development Head of Brandswag, a design and social media communications firm, Author of 'Twitter Marketing for Dummies'

Dedication

To my mother, who forced me to take typing when I didn't want to, and to my son Parker, my first born, and the only other Twitter user in my family (so far). I love them both!

Acknowledgments

Thanks to my family for being my inspiration and providing purpose in my life.

Thanks to my team at The Kevin Eikenberry Group for learning with me and making life a joy.

Thanks to all of our Clients for the opportunity to serve and learn with you.

Thanks to Rajesh Setty (*@upbeatnow*) for inviting me into this project.

Thanks to Chris Brogan for the awesome foreword.

Thanks to all #tweetimonials.

Thanks to you for reading this book.

Thanks to God, for all things (including a book of tweets) are possible through him.

Why I wrote this book?

Leaders are difference makers.
_____

I want to help leaders make a bigger difference.
_____

This book is one part of helping achieve that goal.
_____

Kevin Eikenberry *@KevinEikenberry*

140 Bite-Sized Ideas to Help You Become the Leader You Were Born to Be

Contents

Foreword 13

Section I
Leaders as Learners 17

Section II
Leadership Actions 29

Section III
Leadership Thoughts 67

Section IV
Leadership Inspiration 91

About the Author 105

140 Bite-Sized Ideas to Help You Become the Leader You Were Born to Be

Foreword

Kevin Eikenberry boils leadership down to instruction-packed kernels of action and wisdom. What more could I want?

Chris Brogan *@chrisbrogan*

140 Bite-Sized Ideas to Help You Become the Leader You Were Born to Be

Chris Brogan is the co-author of the bestselling business book, 'Trust Agents.' He is the President of New Marketing Labs, and the Co-founder of PodCamp. Chris writes daily at chrisbrogan.com.

140 Bite-Sized Ideas to Help You Become the Leader You Were Born to Be

# Section 1

Leaders as Learners

Leadership is a complex thing. In order to be good at it, we must continue to learn. In order to develop others, we must model the learning behaviors we want to see in them. The tweets that follow are meant to remind, encourage and challenge you to become the leader you were born to be—and to learn what you need to learn to make that happen.

140 Bite-Sized Ideas to Help You Become the Leader You Were Born to Be

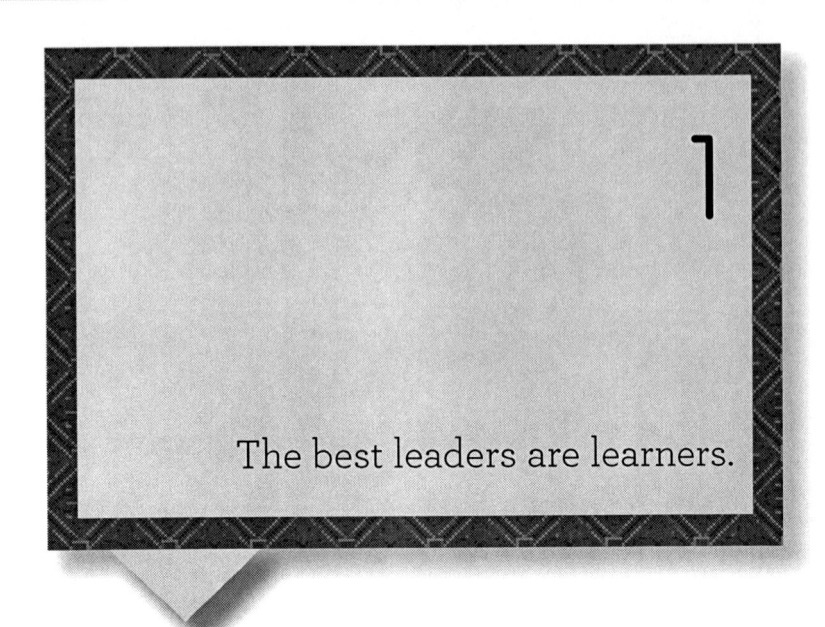

1

The best leaders are learners.

2

Leaders know that to grow learners they must be learners first.

3

Great leaders reflect on their successes and failures, and learn from both.

4

Leaders become remarkable through learning.

5

Remarkable leaders consciously cultivate a learner's mindset.

6

Remarkable leaders are curious leaders.

7

Remarkable leaders don't just learn—they DO something with what they learn!

8

Your ability to observe is your most underappreciated AND underused learning (and leading) skill.

9

Remarkable leaders reflect on their experiences to continue their improvement.

10

Remarkable leaders lead with a learning mindset.

11

Remarkable leaders are curious. Curiosity leads to learning, but only when it is an action that we take every day. How curious are you?

12

Leaders must be in an ongoing learning and practicing mode to become better communicators.

13

Remarkable leaders make mistakes, own them, learn from them, grow from them, and use them as leadership lessons for themselves and others.

14

To learn leadership, you must lead.

15

A great leader is a learning leader.

16

Remarkable leaders know that experience is automatic, but learning is optional. Leaders learn!

17

Remarkable leaders know that all life experiences can help them become better leaders.

#LEADERSHIPtweet

18

Remarkable leaders know there is much to learn, but prioritize one or two focus areas at any given time.

19

Strive to be a leader who learns and a learner who leads.

140 Bite-Sized Ideas to Help You Become the Leader You Were Born to Be

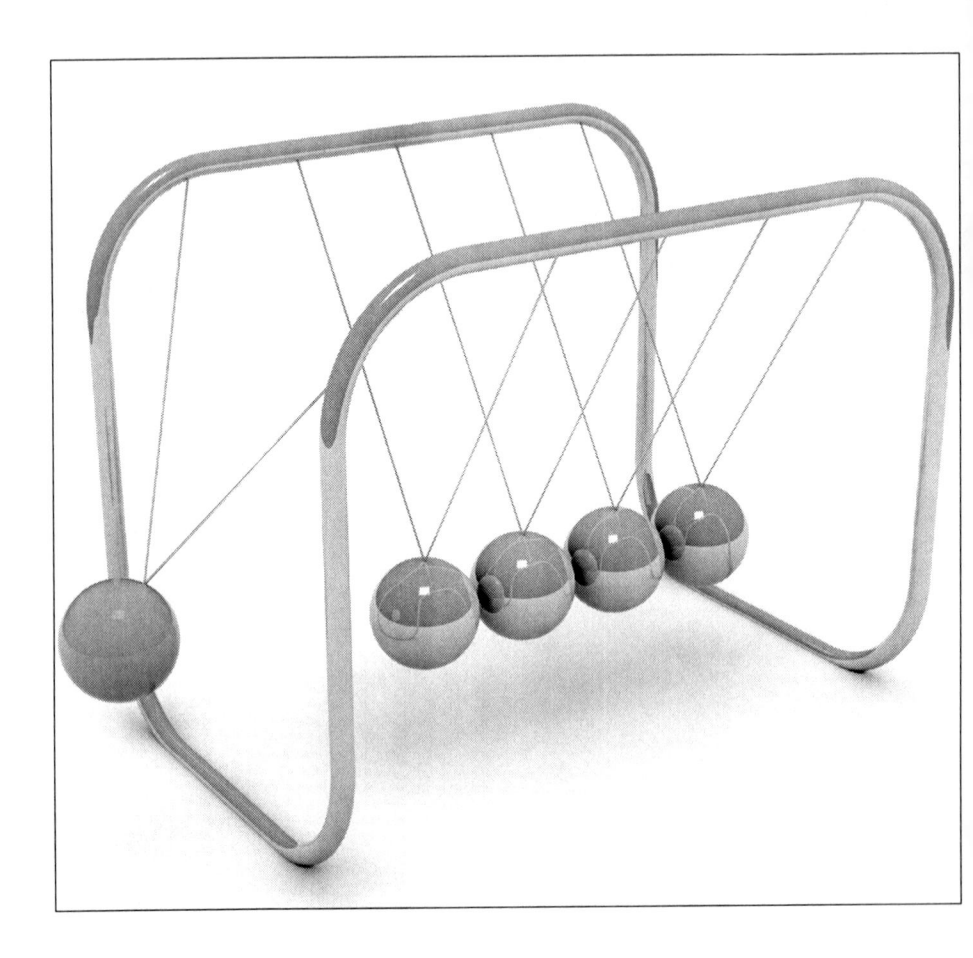

Section II

Leadership Actions

Leadership calls us to action. It isn't a title or a position—it is something we do. To do it well requires not one single thing, but all sorts of actions all the time. In the leader's busy world, sometimes we forget that it isn't about the role or the title, but about the actions. This section offers actions that, when taken, will make a difference in your results.

20

Remarkable leaders have formed a habit of doing things that average leaders don't like to do.

21

When you want higher performance from your team, reward higher performance, coach to higher performance, and expect higher performance.

22

Remarkable leaders create a stronger, more personal vision of change for others.

23

Remarkable leaders clearly see a desired future state and lead others towards it.

24

Remarkable leaders communicate change through conversation, not presentations.

25

Remarkable leaders are change champions.

26

Want to be a leader? Lead! We build any skill through consistent, purposeful practice.

27

Remarkable leaders communicate powerfully through stories.

28

Remarkable leaders hone their listening skills—a powerful habit for better communication.

140 Bite-Sized Ideas to Help You Become the Leader You Were Born to Be

29

Leaders listen to more than the words being said....

30

People don't lead because of their titles. They lead because they chose to use their skills.

31

Creating, fostering, and supporting enjoyment are all ways to create an engaged team.

32

Remarkable leaders are servant leaders.

140 Bite-Sized Ideas to Help You Become the Leader You Were Born to Be

33

Remarkable leaders communicate with others in a way that is best for the other person.

34

Remarkable leaders value creativity and strive to bring out the creative potential of others.

35

Remarkable leaders set short- and long-term goals.

36

Want to communicate more effectively? Adapt your style to the communication habits of the other person.

37
Leaders go first—that is why they are leaders.

38
Remarkable leaders help others set—AND get—their goals.

39

Want to be a better listener? Be less selfish and more curious.

40

Remarkable leaders are accountable for their actions.

41

Remarkable leaders believe in the potential of those they lead.

42

Remarkable leaders build the confidence levels of others.

140 Bite-Sized Ideas to Help You Become the Leader You Were Born to Be

43

Remarkable leaders are willing to make bold decisions.

44

Remarkable leaders set healthy, yet expansive, expectations.

45

Remarkable leaders view failure, properly reflected on, as a precursor to success.

46

Remarkable leaders go for their goals and support others in doing the same.

47

Remarkable leaders have a bias for action—sometimes they know you must just do it!

48

Remarkable leaders are nurturers—they nurture ideas, plans, teams, others—and themselves.

#LEADERSHIP**tweet**

49

Remarkable leaders plan for, prepare for, and project success.

50

Remarkable leaders are open to input from others—they care more about results than getting credit.

51

Remarkable leaders keep promises—
to themselves and their followers.

52

Remarkable leaders see their teams—
and themselves—as winners!

53

Remarkable leaders work to master the fundamentals of human behavior and communication.

140 Bite-Sized Ideas to Help You Become the Leader You Were Born to Be

54

Lead is a verb—it is something you DO.

55

Leaders are believers—they believe in themselves, their team, and possibilities!

56

Remarkable leaders make others more successful. How are you making others great today?

57

Remarkable leaders are planters. They plant ideas, people, and visions. What are you planting?

140 Bite-Sized Ideas to Help You Become the Leader You Were Born to Be

58

Leaders look to the future—expectantly, hopefully, actively, and often. And after they look, they take action!

59

Remarkable leaders ask important questions.

#LEADERSHIP**tweet**

60

Remarkable leaders take actions that serve others.

61

Remarkable leaders aren't perfect, but they are role models.

62

Remarkable leaders are great dreamers and massive doers.

63

Remarkable leaders need to focus the team on something positive, uplifting, and productive.

64

Remarkable leaders help their teams align their goals in support of the larger organizational goals.

65

Remarkable leaders are skilled question askers.

66

Remarkable leaders work with others to co-create goals.

67

Remarkable leaders translate vision into reality.

68

Remarkable leaders know that they are responsible for creating goal alignment.

69

Remarkable leaders talk *with* people rather than *to* them.

70

Remarkable leaders "make work play" for themselves and others.

71

Remarkable leaders prioritize based on the biggest goals and most precious values.

72

Trust is the currency of relationships. Remarkable leaders work to build it every day.

73

Remarkable leaders are network builders.

74

Remarkable leaders lead from their values.

75

Remarkable leaders are great mentors and facilitate learning for those they mentor.

76

Remarkable leaders achieve their goals faster through the help of their ever-expanding network.

77

Remarkable leaders encourage people to be innovative, creative, and productive.

78

Remarkable leaders do more than manage projects—they lead them.

79

Remarkable leaders support and enable process improvement.

80

Remarkable leaders repeat what works AND look for improvements and breakthroughs too.

81

Remarkable leaders engage others in their vision, goals, and direction.

140 Bite-Sized Ideas to Help You Become the Leader You Were Born to Be

Section III

Leadership Thoughts

If you want to be a better leader, you must think. Yes, leadership, as you were reminded in the last section, requires action, but it also requires that we think. Take some time and think about the ideas that follow. They will help you learn and take better action in the future.

140 Bite-Sized Ideas to Help You Become the Leader You Were Born to Be

82

The status quo requires no leadership.

83

Change is the currency of leadership.

84

People don't resist change; they resist being changed.

85

Leaders realize resistance is not inherently negative nor does it need to be squelched; rather, it is naturally occurring and should be valued/explored.

86

Better feedback starts with a clear intention.

87

Remarkable leaders know that it is impossible to over-communicate.

88

Want to improve your communication skills? Remember that you can't NOT communicate. What are you communicating?

140 Bite-Sized Ideas to Help You Become the Leader You Were Born to Be

89

Resistance is energy that leaders use to move their change forward.

90

Want your message to be heard and remembered? Tell a compelling story.

91

The most effective presentations are focused on the needs and desires of the audience.

92

Strong working relationships are a sign of leadership strength.

93

Effective listening isn't about technique. It is about caring about the speaker and the message.

94

Remarkable leaders are likable leaders (though not all their decisions are liked).

95

Stories are a powerful way to create connections and common understanding.

96

Creative ideas are required to craft the future results leaders desire.

97

Confidence is a bigger key to performance than most consider—but effective leaders do more than consider it—they build it.

98

Remarkable leaders have a healthy self-image.

99

Remarkable leaders innovate because they know the future will require new ideas!

100

Be authentic—you will be a more successful leader (and person).

101

Are leaders born or made? Yes! We take our natural gifts AND apply them to the important work of leadership, improving through practice.

102

Mentoring is more than just giving advice—great mentors are invested in the success of their protégés and operate in dialogue.

140 Bite-Sized Ideas to Help You Become the Leader You Were Born to Be

103

"How can we make it work?"—a great leadership question.

104

A leadership success test—when you leave, others are ready to lead.

105

Remarkable leaders are willing to look silly if it supports their team and their vision.

106

Remarkable leaders aren't fire fighters; they are fire preventers.

107

Remarkable leaders focus on the future, live in the present, and learn from the past.

108

Remarkable leaders know that the best thing to say might be a question, a statement or explanation, or nothing.

109

Remarkable leaders are like farmers—they plant seeds of vision, encouragement and support, and reap results, growth, and success.

110

Want better ideas? Create MORE ideas.

111

Remarkable leaders focus more on expectation than inspection, on reflection more than exhortation.

112

Remarkable leaders know that serving customers is everyone's job.

113

Remarkable leaders know that empowerment is a two-way street.

114

Remarkable leaders structure their teams based on the needs of the work, not on a preconceived notion of team greatness.

#LEADERSHIP**tweet**

115

Remarkable leaders know that a mistake is a great chance to improve a customer relationship.

116

Remarkable leaders know that attitude is contagious and choose the one they want to spread.

117

Want to increase your sphere of influence? Serve more!

118

While leadership and management are different, the best leaders are effective managers too.

119

Remarkable leaders know the importance of fun for themselves and those they lead.

120

Martin Luther King, Jr. was a leader with a dream. What is your dream?

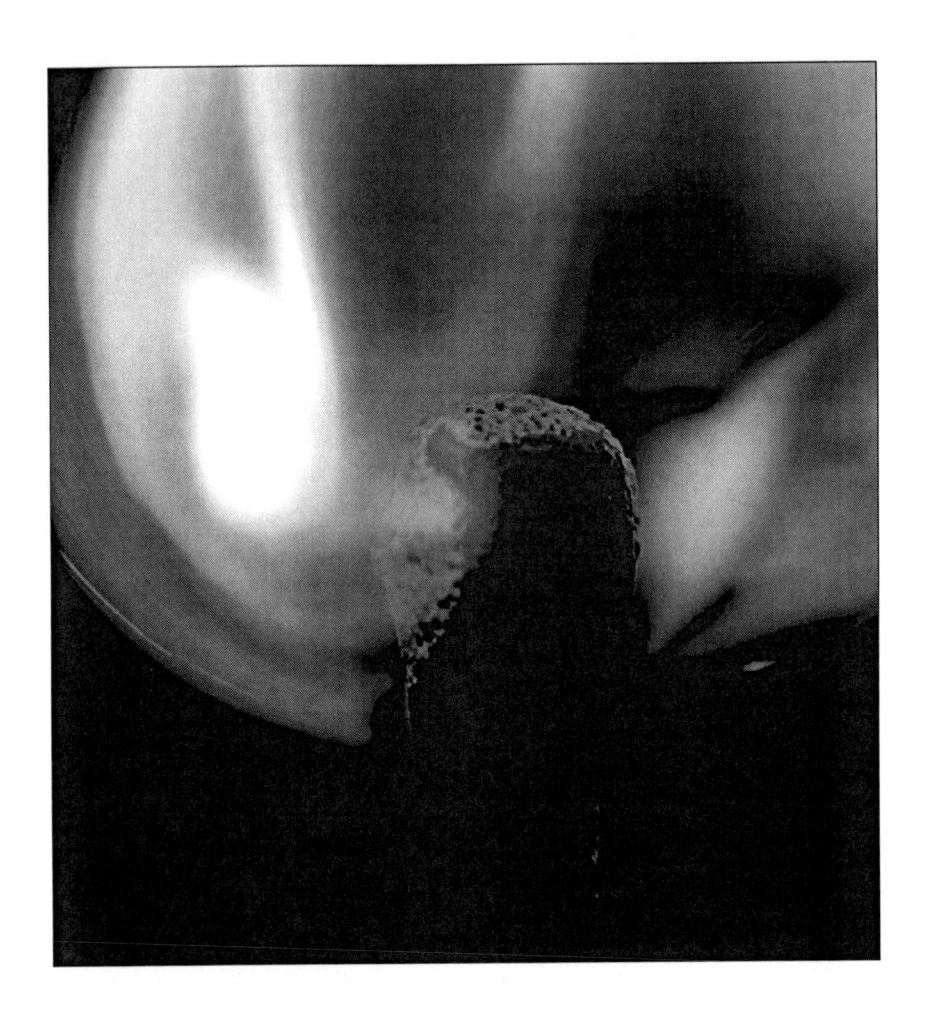

140 Bite-Sized Ideas to Help You Become the Leader You Were Born to Be

Section IV

Leadership Inspiration

Leadership is rewarding but hard work. To be our best we must be inspired. To bring out the best in others we must be inspiring. The ideas that follow were written with these twin facts in mind. Read on and be inspired!

140 Bite-Sized Ideas to Help You Become the Leader You Were Born to Be

121

Great leaders must inspire others to act, so they must remain personally inspired. How are you being inspired today?

122

Make a choice to make a difference. Make a choice to lead.

123

People can choose to change, to get on board, to engage. As leaders, we help them make those choices.

124

Leaders: Please listen to Peter Drucker—"The best way to predict your future is to create it." Remarkable leaders don't wait. They create!

125

Great listening starts with an open heart and a curious mind.

126

As we become better leaders, we become better human beings (and vice versa).

127

Remarkable leaders passionately believe in the potential of other people.

128

Work. Play. Lead. (Three important things or just one thing?)

129

Work. Play. Lead. Learn. Love. (And the boundaries can go away.)—Thanks *@AngieChaplin* for the addition!

130

Remarkable leaders are on a constant quest for a better future for those they lead and the world around them.

131

Leaders aren't all-knowing or perfect—they are genuine and are genuinely leading others towards a desired future.

132

Remarkable leaders contemplate the beauty of the future they are moving towards.

133

Persistence matters for matters of personal achievement and leadership.

134

Remarkable leaders strive to be their best selves most of the time, each day.

135

Your belief in someone's potential is the first step towards helping them develop it.

136

Remarkable leaders know that any interaction can be a development opportunity—for both parties.

137

Remarkable leaders choose to positively impact organizational culture, regardless of their job title.

138

Remarkable leaders know there are opportunities to practice leadership in every area of their lives.

139

Remarkable leadership starts with a belief that leadership skills are learnable and learned.

140

Leadership is an opportunity and a responsibility. The best leaders accept both realities.

140 Bite-Sized Ideas to Help You Become the Leader You Were Born to Be

About the Author

Kevin Eikenberry is the Chief Potential Officer of The Kevin Eikenberry Group (http://KevinEikenberry.com), a learning consulting company that provides a wide range of services, including training delivery and design facilitation, performance coaching, organizational consulting, and speaking services.

He speaks, consults, trains, coaches, and writes on leadership, organizational, professional, and personal development.

He is the bestselling author of 'Remarkable Leadership—Unleashing Your Leadership Potential One Skill at a Time' and 'Vantagepoints on Learning and Life,' and a contributor to over 20 other books. He writes two blogs—*Remarkable Learning* (http://kevineikenberry.com/blogs/index.asp) and *Unleashing Your Leadership Potential* (http://tinyurl.com/yj7v7bo).

He is the creator of over 200 leadership and learning products, including the **Remarkable Leadership Learning System** (http://Remarkable-Leadership.com), and has created the **Most Remarkable Free Leadership Gift Ever** (http://tinyurl.com/yhee5hx).